You're reading God bless!

# Diamonds of the Dawn

## Christian Reflection

### by

### Byron von Rosenberg

*Diamonds of the Dawn*
Copyright © 2017 Byron von Rosenberg
All rights reserved

Cover design by Heather von Rosenberg
Interior design by Sharon von Rosenberg

Published by
Red Mountain Creations
P. O. Box 172
High Ridge, MO  63049
www.idontwanttokissallama.com
redmountain@swbell.net
1-866-SEA-GULS

Publisher's Cataloging-in-Publication Data
provided by Five Rainbows Cataloging Services

Names: von Rosenberg, Byron.

Title: Diamonds of the dawn : Christian reflection / Byron von Rosenberg.
Description: Byrnes Mill, MO : Red Mountain Creations, 2017.

Identifiers: ISBN 978-0-9910804-2-7 (hardcover)

Subjects: LCSH: Christian poetry, American. | Religious poetry. | Jesus Christ--Poetry.
  | Christian life. | Love. | BISAC: POETRY / Subjects & Themes / Inspirational &
  Religious.
  | RELIGION / Christian Life / Inspirational. | RELIGION / Christianity / Literature
  & the Arts.

Classification:     LCC PS3622.O57 D53 2017 (print)
                    | LCC PS3622.O57 (ebook) | DDC 811\.6--dc23.

**Printed in the United States of America** by Bang Printing, Brainerd, MN.

*Diamonds of the Dawn*
*is dedicated to my mother*


*Marjorie Taylor von Rosenberg*


*An alphabeticdal list of poems begins on page 142.*

**Byron von Rosenberg** is the author of eleven children's and poetry books. He is a regular storyteller at Grant's Farm in St. Louis and has spoken at many schools and churches. Byron began his creative career with bedtime stories to his children, Ryan and Erin, and started writing poetry in 2002 with a poem for his father, Dale. He earned his B.S. degree in Chemical Engineering from the University of Tulsa in 1979 and a Masters in Human Services from Murray State University. Byron is the *poet laureate* of Byrnes Mill, Missouri where he lives with his wife, Sharon.

**Heather von Rosenberg** is a native of Leicester in the United Kingdom and earned a B.A. degree in Illustration from Lincoln University. Her art is displayed on the cover of this book, in two of Byron's children's books and on the web at www.facebook.com/sugarcatillustration. She is married to the author's son, Ryan.

# DIAMONDS OF THE DAWN

Windows, windshields, water,
every piece of sparkling glass
shining bright like diamonds
as the sun makes its morning pass –
All across the valley
to the top of farthest hills
light overflows the sun
and onto earth it spills.
It reflects off of the puddles
the rain left yesterday
and glistens upon the bottle cap
that someone threw away.
These things so common, worthless,
and I would pay no mind
but the light that shines from each of them
almost makes me blind.
For no matter how they started out
they shine when shined upon
and all of us, God's children,
are diamonds of the dawn.

# ON BLUEBONNET HILL

I remember climbing
the bluebonnet hill
on a cool spring day
when the morning air was still.
Like a giant wave it rose
as from the deep blue sea,
the beauty of the earth that God
had chosen just for me.
And from atop that giant wave
I held my arms above
surrounded by the evidence
of God's abounding love.
All who gathered with me
stood silently in awe
and recollect to this day
the splendor that we saw.
It's a place and time I go
when pain and hate surround
for they have no dominion here.
It's my Father's hallowed ground.
And for its many blessings
share it fully now I do
so you may also walk with God
in that field of blue.

# IN THE SUDDEN SILENCE

I spend so much time talking
to get my point across
to my wife and children
and sometimes to my boss.
I tried to talk to God
this morning as I prayed
but with the dawn's new grandeur
my lips and tongue were stayed.
And in the sudden silence
I heard the new day born
from the chatter of the birds
to an angry driver's horn.
The laughter of some children
who ran outside to play,
the sound of my own breathing,
yes, I heard that today.
And I think I heard the sunrise
through space so far away
for God can tell me anything
when I listen as I pray.
and I pray that I
am still, as HE speaks
to me today.

## SECRETLY SPINNING

Secretly spinning
from time's beginning
the earth sings a song to me.
It's everywhere
in the movement of air
as it plays with each leaf on the tree.
So listen ye well
for there are stories to tell
that no human voice can relay
for there's a spirit that flows
in the wind as it blows
and I hear it so clearly today.
And I wish that I could
take this song from the wood
and sing it for each one of you.
But it carries not
and the words I forgot
so your own attending you'll just have to do.
Yet I know if you'll listen
as the winter stars glisten
you'll hear the song the earth plays.
It's a tune you will know
as the soft breezes blow
giving God all glory and praise.

## NO LOOKING BACK

No looking back at life
and wondering what I've missed.
Not one single thing
on my bucket list.
No, I haven't done it all
nor made the hall of fame
but there are accomplishments
that I alone can claim.
I listened to the Voice of God
Who answered when I prayed
and walked into the shadows
of the valley unafraid.
I learned that riches are not found
in sacks filled up with gold
but rather in performance
of deeds and actions bold.
God gave me a companion
whom I completely trust
and love that will endure
when all else turns to dust.
And the reason that I say
I've done all I came to do
is He showed me the Promised Land
and let me walk with you.

# THE FORGOTTEN GIFT

He put it on his Christmas list
when he was just a boy
and he prayed to Jesus often
for this gift was not a toy.
For many years he sought it
but it was never there
and sometimes he grew bitter.
It just did not seem fair.
There were many things to do.
The boy became a man.
The gift he asked for he forgot
but Jesus had a plan.
"Lose your life for me.
Treat others as yourself."
When the man had done these things
his gift came off the shelf.
And now he walks in wonder,
a smile of joy upon his face.
He got the gift he asked for.
Jesus gave him grace.

# GRACE IS

Grace is putting smiles
on undeserving faces.
Grace is being first
and after, trading places.
Grace is knowing Jesus
and sharing His embraces.
Seeing Him in everything,
that's what God's true Grace is.

Grace is time alone
with God in open spaces.
Grace is sharing Jesus
with all people and all races.
Grace is blessed assurance,
doubt dispersed that leaves no traces.
The faith that's in a mustard seed,
yes friend, that's what God's Grace is.

Grace is going joyfully
through life's varied paces.
Grace is running with a dream
that's worthy of the chases.
Grace is letting God
be your whole life's basis.
Jesus' love that frees the world
is what God's Holy Grace is.

## IT TOOK YOU

What manner of being are you
with eyes so bright and true
whose cry awakens me at night
then quiets soft when I'm in sight?
How have you in such short stead
come to own my heart and head?
In time all things must end they say
but not our love I hope and pray
for in this moment I hold dear
the love of God He's posted near
touching me with little hands
so now this lost one understands
the joy of love God finds in me.

It took you, Child,
so I could see.

Sharon and I dreamed of opening a store called **The Forgotten Gift**
in Branson, Missouri. We later opened the **I Don't Want to Kiss
a Llama!** store in the St. Louis area and ran it for six years.
"It Took You" was written at the store in Crestwood, Missouri.

# LIKE NO OTHER

As gentle as an ocean breeze
that lulls the sun to sleep,
more constant than resplendent stars
reflected in the deep,
dazzling like the summer sun
that garbs the earth in green,
her beauty's like a velvet rose
that bids to touch once seen.
Soft as celestial pillows
as they drift across the sky
yet ferocious as a lioness
should she hear her young ones cry.
Swift as a gazelle
to fill their every need
so her children shine as diamonds
in thought and word and deed.
Unique in all the cosmos,
a creation like no other,
unblemished love from heaven's heights
refined on earth is mother.

I wrote "Diamonds of the Dawn" after a sunrise walk
on the hill near my home in Byrnes Mill, Missouri
on April 4, 2003.

# LOOK AT MY HANDS

Look at my hands, now crippled and old.
Once so strong, now what can they hold?

THEY HOLD THE LOVE
I GAVE TO YOU.
YOU PASSED IT ON
YET IT STAYED AND GREW.

I felt it, Dad, when you held me high.
I laughed and sang and touched the sky.
I felt God's love when you passed it through
and now I'm here to bring it back to you.

Look at my feet! I can barely stand.
They climbed tall mountains and crossed the land!

THEY CARRY THE MESSAGE
OF JESUS' LOVE
HIGHER THAN MOUNTAINTOPS
TO HEAVEN ABOVE.

I followed you, Dad, to that highest peak
and I followed you, Dad, our Savior to seek.
Your feet led me to Him when I was a boy.
With Him in our hearts, each day's filled with joy.

It's so hard to breathe! The air is so thin.
I want to shout and sing praises again.

I STILL HEAR THE SONGS
AND THE PRAISES YOU LIFT!
COME SING THEM IN HEAVEN
WHERE NEW LIFE IS YOUR GIFT.

You taught me to sing, Dad. With you I give praise
and I thank God today I was your son to raise.
All of your family and your many friends, too,
each of us, all of us, see Jesus in you.

He's my Daddy, Lord. I can't say good-bye!
Whatever you do, please don't let him die!

THE LOVE THAT I GAVE HIM
HE PASSED ON TO YOU.
NOW PASS IT TO OTHERS
AND WATCH IT RENEW.

Don't fret over me, son. I've been born again!
I'm living in heaven and free from all sin.
My hands are strong! My feet can run!
Hear me shout, "Hallelujah! The victory's won!"

Written for my father, Dale,
on June 24, 2002.

## ONE KISS FOR ALL THE ROSES

I offer you a yellow rose
to catch the sun's bright rays
but it's the laughter of your heart
that adds sparkle to my days.
I offer you a pure white rose
like silver snow so soft
for as snowflakes ride upon the breeze
so love keeps us aloft.
I offer you a sweet pink rose,
luxurious, inviting,
for it's the chance to be with you
that makes my life exciting.
I offer you a deep red rose
to symbolize my heart
for it is yours as well
as this new life we start.
I offer you one single kiss
for a rose of every hue,
one kiss for all the roses
as I give my love to you.

My mother loves roses and my dad loved her.

# LEAVES AT THANKSGIVING

Leaves at Thanksgiving
on trees are so few
most of them resting
on the ground like the dew.
An offering of gold
laid down by the tree,
holding back nothing
it gives thankfully.
And naked and barren
it faces the chill,
sure God's love never ends
though the winter's cold will.
And I realize in watching
that if I, too, were so sure
there is nothing so awful
I could not endure.
And that if I would give thanks,
my own offering bring,
God's gifts would be countless
like new leaves in the spring.

Inspired by an otherwise ordinary tree
in Forest Park in St. Louis on November 22, 2004.

## JUST ANOTHER CHRISTMAS

It's just another Christmas
with gifts and mistletoe,
just another winter's day
that I'll be shoveling snow.
But I'll pour a cup of chocolate,
sit by the fire to warm my feet,
then surrounded by the ones I love
share something good to eat.
I'll listen to their laughter
and watch the firelight dance.
If it's just another Christmas
how does it so entrance?
Is it music from the angels
singing high above
bringing forth the best in us
with the best of gifts, God's love?
Just another ordinary
yet special Christmas Day
with tender thoughts of you
and with you in mind we pray.
His Blessings for the coming year
our Christmas wish for you,
and as we listen to the angels
we hope you hear them, too.

## THE GIFT OF THE HEART OF GOD

Lord I ask only
please give me Your heart
so my eyes may see fully,
not just in part.
Give me Your heart
so these my own hands
no longer heed earthly
but heaven's commands.
Give me Your heart
so these feet I call mine
find and then follow
pathways divine.
Give me Your heart
so each thought is a prayer
and each moment a chance
to show how deeply I care.
Give me Your heart
for therein is the Light
to conquer the darkness
and make the world bright.
Conquer my fears
with Your heart in my chest
and my pride when I'm thinking
it's me who knows best.
Give me Your heart, Lord,
and humility, too,
so the Love of Your Spirit
may always pass through.
Give me Your heart
so there's nothing I lack
and I'll spend my whole life
giving it back.

# ON THIS DAY

If I should shiver on this day
it will not be in fear
for Jesus has fulfilled
His promise – and He's here.
And should I hunger on this day
it will not be for bread
but for the Word of God
by which my soul is fed.
And should I dream I shall dream
of comfort, love and peace
and pray and work to see
that each of these increase.
On this day I shall give thanks
whatever may befall
knowing that God loves me
and His children one and all.
And when this day is over
I will feel no sorrow
for God Who gives me bread today
provides again tomorrow.

My mother is an author and artist. She has painted
the bluebonnets since falling in love with them
when she moved to Texas in 1953. She told me
the story of "The Bluebonnet Hill" in October of 2016.

# AND JESUS TOUCHED . . .

And Jesus touched a hammer
to build beauty out of wood.
Joseph taught him well
and Jesus' skills were good.
He could have lived a quiet life
making things this way
but Jesus felt a stirring
and went outside to pray.
And the heavens opened to Him,
God's one and only Son.
Today the world is different
for what He's said and done.
And Jesus touched a hammer
one last time with care
before He stepped outside his shop
into the morning air.

And Jesus touched a leper,
the blind, the sick, the lame,
all of them God's children
and He loved them just the same.
He could have spent a joyous life
helping folks this way
but there was more to do,
a debt for us to pay.
For as hearts were opened to Him
He sought to set them free
and still He seeks the same
to do for you and me.
And Jesus touched a leper
who instantly was cured.
God, let me too, trust Jesus
my healing thus assured.

And Jesus touched a cup
and passed it all around
so that all who drink of it
may one day be found.

He could have spent the evening
safely in that place
but He went out to the garden
to meet God face to face.
And as enemies appeared to Him
He did not run in fear.
He knew the test was coming
and His time was drawing near.
And Jesus took the cup
and drank it unafraid.
God, thank You so for Jesus
who for my life did trade.

And Jesus touched a nail
as they drove it through His hand.
He did that for me
and I just can't understand.
He could have spent eternity
in heaven with You, Lord,
but He hung upon a cross
and its cruelty endured.
He saw the heavens open
and You waiting there above
yet He chose to die for me
and save me with His love.
And Jesus touched a nail
through His hand so cruelly thrust.
God, I place my hope in Jesus
and in His Name I trust.

And Jesus touched my heart
and called me as His own.
His love's the greatest power
this world has ever known.
And I can spend eternity
singing joy and praises
since Jesus broke death's grip
and all believers raises.
For I see the heavens open!
He stands there at the gate!

Give your life to Him right now.
This is no time to wait!
For Jesus touches all
who ask this simple prayer,
"Come into my heart, dear Lord,
and make Your home right there."

I read this poem on KJ SL radio in St. Louis
when they had the Tim and Al show in the mornings.

# A DOZEN SEASHELLS

A dozen little seashells
scooped up on the beach,
if I wash them and look closely
there's beauty found in each:
The way one feels against my skin,
how it glistens in the light,
the color of the ocean
or pitch of black at night.
One is old and broken,
another alive and new,
together for an instant
in this time we're walking through.
And what of all the people
who play in ocean swells?
Are they not as beautiful
as the sunlight on the shells?
It amazes me that God has made
every shell and grain of sand
and takes the time to look at me
and hold me in His hand.

Inspired by a trip to the beach
and written on December 12, 2003.

# I AM SAMPSON

I am Sampson as he writhes
in cruel humiliation
whose suffering is seen by all
to be his own creation.
He prayed for strength to topple
the house of Philistines
causing his own death!
Revenge by any means!
His tale lives on for contrast
of his strength and woes.
I wage a battle just as fierce
and yet nobody knows.
I thank the Lord for Sampson
who showed what strength can do
and ask Him for the power
this next day to get through.
Not to hate but love
those who do me wrong!
Not for strength of limb
but in Spirit to be strong!
And remembered in a poem
in the midst of battle writ
recounting that to hatred's lure
I did not submit.

## ESAU'S BOW

He had carried the distance before
when he was hunting game.
"If I loose the arrow now
the result will be the same."
There was satisfaction
in the stretching bow
and he could end his suffering
with just a single blow.
The gifts had been delivered,
sheep and oxen, goats,
and the pleas of singing voices
joined the lyre's soft notes.
Jacob's seed not his
would be written in the book,
these the thoughts in Esau's head
as the fatal aim he took.
"Better than a deer
with innocence of eye,
more than any wolf
he deserves to die."
He felt the anger fill him
as many times before.
"Let the arrow go
and I shall hurt no more!"
Then upon his shoulder
he felt a gentle hand,
a voice to him familiar
and her words, "I understand."
"You can have a life with me
if you let the arrow go
but better in a million ways
if you set down your bow."
He felt the soft hand slide
and the footsteps fall away.
"He stole from me! I'll kill him!"
he heard his anger say.
"Loving and forgiveness
received and not returned

yet once more given freely
is a godly lesson learned."
"Go into the shadows
and cry deep from your soul!
Cast out your grief and anger
and God will make you whole."
He lowered just a little
the arrow's tip of stone
and felt again the joy of heart
that as a boy he'd known.
He set the bow down quickly
and the tension from the string.
Freed from all its demons
his heart began to sing.
"I will harbor hatred
not a moment longer.
I choose peace for both of us.
It matters not who's stronger.
For stronger far than we
is He who rules the skies!"
And thus said Jacob's brother
whose pain had made him wise.

# BELONGING

I am being forced to move
from what was once my home
and told that like a gypsy
my job is now to roam.
I have been belonging
to a place of peace
where quiet contemplation
understanding did increase.
Here I have collected
things I value much.
Life it seems is made
oftentimes of such.
Is it God or man who says,
"Put these things away!"?
Should I cry or celebrate
as I start this day?
I shall shed a tear
for here I did belong
and will endure and prosper
for God has made me strong!
What is more important,
a concept or a place?
Each in its own time
leads a man to Grace.
The thought, "He's coming with me!"
causes me to smile.
With God as my companion
I'll treasure every mile!
I lift mine eyes unto the hills
and raise my hands above.
I belong to God and so
I leave this place I love.

# A PERFECT ROSE

Taken from the garden
it was a perfect rose
and still the same in vase.
Does it matter where one grows?
It can still be perfect
despite life's highs and lows
because it has a purpose
and it's the one God chose.
And though I have been tattered
and torn by many throes
for the love of Jesus
I am one of those.

My mother picked a perfect rose as a schoolgirl
in Cambridge Massachusetts. Her teacher displayed it
for a week.  Mom told me about it in October of 2016.

# HEART ENOUGH

Heart enough to find the good
that others cannot see
and help a person to become
who God would have them be.
Heart enough to make the climb
where others will not go
and then return to lend a hand,
the upward way to show.
Heart enough to stand against
the fiercest winter storm
and build a fire of kindness
to keep His children warm.
Heart enough to look beyond
the dark and dreary sky
knowing God will lift me up
if first I dare to try.
Heart enough to give my all
and proclaim Him to the end
for eternity is mine
with Jesus as my friend!
Grant me courage, my dear Lord,
when the times I face are tough
so that like You upon the cross
I may have heart enough.

# HORSES ON HILLSIDES

Horses on hillsides
with grass growing green
and bright sky above
the bluest I've seen,
sure signs that spring
is ready to start
and here is another:
The leap of my heart!
For there's something so special
about such a place
that wherever you are
brings a smile to your face.
There's a feeling I get
from hillsides and horses
for I'm somehow connected
to God's natural forces.
They shine in the blue
and the sunlight above
and in horses on hillsides
that speak of His love.

There was a special place near the highway
where Sharon and I would look for the horses
on our way to Branson from St. Louis and back.

# I WOULD WAIT A THOUSAND YEARS

I would wait a thousand years
but You'd have me speak today.
Thank You, Lord, for granting me
the privilege to pray.
I would walk a thousand miles
to show my love for You
and yet it's here inside my heart
the greatest work to do.
I would sail the ocean
and cross a thousand seas
and yet You give me everything
when I ask it on my knees.
I would die a thousand times
yet You want me to live
for when He died for me
You did all my sins forgive.
And so I'll live each single day
amazed at what You've done
giving thanks a thousand times
for Jesus, Your own Son.

I wrote "Secretly Spinning" on
December 20, 2004 at a picnic table
at Creve Coeur Park during lunch hour .
It was very cold so I did not wait.

# MY SECOND CHANCE

I had a dream this morning
that I had a second chance
to do love the right way
and the cause of truth advance.
And it seemed to me that if
I could get that break
I'd change my life forever!
What a different path I'd take.
But just before my chance
to change my life arose
my dream began to fade
as I woke up from my doze.
Disappointment wracked
both my heart and mind.
I'd never get that second chance!
To that I was resigned.
But then the notion hit me
and I chuckled in surprise!
I have that chance today
when I see the sun arise.
I can change today
and I know the way to start:
Treat my neighbor as myself
and love God with all my heart.

# I AM AN IMAGE

The greatest cure and greatest curse
on this grain of sand
is man's supposed capacity
to learn and understand.
For we are so concerned
with "how to that and this?"
that we focus on the finer points
whilst larger things we miss.
We have eaten fruit
from the knowledge tree
but put us all together
and our capacity
is not enough to cure the ills
that drive us to our graves.
Only Jesus frees us
from death that makes us slaves.
He has freed me many times
and doubtless will again
because I fall into the traps
that Satan sets for men.
I like to think what I have learned
will surely save the day
but pride keeps me from finding
the good and narrow way.
Made I am an image
of my God above
yet truly I am nothing
if I have not love.
For it is love not knowledge
alone that sets me free
and Jesus' grace that opens
my once blind eyes to see.

# AT THE BEGINNING

Like a seagull o'er the ocean
cries out because it's free
I am witness to God's creation
and it's all beautiful to me.
Like a rose in springtime
opens to the sun
so God would make us all
before His work is done.
Like the love I feel
when I look into your eyes
God's miracles abound
and fill us with surprise.
Like the first step on a journey
at the beginning of the day
my life is starting over
as Jesus leads the way.
And where that journey leads me
it matters not at all
for the greatest joy in any life
is answering His call.

I wrote the poem "True Friends" for my friend
and travelling companion  Joe Galbraith  when we moved
from Corpus Christi in 1992. That poem was published
in **Don't Feed the Seagulls** in 2002.

## WONDERS OF WISDOM

When Jesus prayed,
"God spare me this task!"
He sought only mercy.
It was no sin to ask.
Mercy deserved
undoubtedly so
yet when the time came
He was willing to go.
So why, I do wonder,
that whenever I'm
afraid and ask mercy
it's considered a crime?
Undeserved mercy
and yet mercy still –
isn't this, too,
a part of God's will?
They say all I'm doing
is running from pain
but to run towards it instead
is clearly insane.
Even Christ asked
His Father in prayer
if there were room in His will
His suffering to spare.
And knowing the answer
He accepted His fate.
He took on His task
never yielding to hate.
"Forgive me my sins
and spare me!" I cry.
God does this for me!
Why can't man try?
Mercy and love
in abundance God rains
yet when passes through man
so little remains.
Mercy denied!
Yes, I know it too well

but I hear God's voice calling
as clear as a bell.
"Give unto others
what they've denied you.
Courage I render
such great deeds to do.
Trust in My power
not in your own.
This is how wonders
of wisdom are grown."

I wrote the poem "Look at My Hands" at my brother
Clyde's house in 2002. I asked God to send me His words
as I had none of my own. Then my niece Karen found
a yellow pad for me to write on. It was the beginning.

.

# A BUTTERFLY IN RUINS

A momentary life
amongst the broken stones
the butterfly in ruins
gleams in teeming tones.
From place to place it flutters
and everywhere it goes
the castle that is rubble
for an instant glows.
And I wonder if the butterfly
fears for anything
for now the ruined butterfly
has but a single wing.
No amount of money
can make it fly again.
Will e're another butterfly
venture where it's been?
The lonely wing is beating
throbbing as my heart
which like the ruined butterfly
is wholly torn apart.
Stupid butterfly
that among the ruins dies!
Stupid, stupid heart
that loud in anguish cries!

# NOTHING LOST

The world seems full of people
resolved to do destruction
usually in secret.
They give no introduction.
They do their work in mystery
of hidden heart and mind
oftentimes resolved
to destroy by acting kind.
How am I to guard the ones
who I love so much
when I can't feel the evil
in the slayer's touch?
Who can I depend on
when my own wisdom fails?
God and God alone
for He alone prevails!
He will set our feet upon
the path that leads to Grace
for there is nothing lost
that it cannot replace.

I see a connection between these two poems
though they were written almost a year apart.

## NO RESTING PLACE

There is no resting place
on this road that I have taken
as in pursuit of heavenly
I've earthly things forsaken.
For the hunger in my belly
is not for meat and bread
but for the Word of God.
I live on that instead.
And when my body aches
and cries in lack or pain
His Spirit gives me comfort
that I cannot explain.
The knowledge that He holds me
safely in His palm
though lost I seem in wilderness
renders peace and calm.
No place to lay my head
nor soothe my tired feet
yet God provides for me
a resting place complete.
And I marvel and I wonder
at all that I behold –
a wilderness transformed
into streets of gold.

## NOW COMES THE GLORY

First on the hill
in the tallest of trees
on the uppermost bough
where the early bird sees
one shining ray,
an answer to prayer,
that lights on the earth
to say God is there.
And lightens my heart
from which hope had been torn
for up with the dawn
the dream is reborn.
And opens my eyes
so at last I can see
how many times
God's done this for me.
All of creation
for a moment is still
in awe for the presence
of God on the hill.

Then touches the land,
the flowers and grass
where soon now the feet
of my neighbors will pass.
People I see
but still do not know,
just as for me,
God shines where they go.
And shines in my heart
which I had supposed
so long in the dark
would forever be closed.
And opens my eyes
so I, too, can see
that all of His children
are important to me.
All of creation

stirs with His hand
moving in concert
as it touches the land.

Last in the shadows
to dry up the dew
and transform into joy
what sorrow once knew,
a soul lost in darkness
never to shine
yet still He can reach
for His light is divine.
And reaches my heart!
"Hallelujah!" I sing
as the hosts in the heavens
and on earth all take wing.
And lifting my eyes
to the brightening sky
so does my spirit
also leap high
as all of creation
from the first to the last
hail Him as King
of both compact and vast.

Now comes the glory
of God in His day
when every transgression
is swept clean away.
Inside of His children
He places His light
filling their hearts
with the love that is might.
And stretches my heart
and my hands open wide
spilling the light
and the love from inside.
And eyes that can see,
not for light but with grace,
are able at last

to ponder His face.
All of creation
from that face doeth flow
and join in the praise
of the Savior I know.

So awake ye now gently.
He's calling to you.
Deep in your heart
you know what to do.
The light that is melting
the dew drops away
signals the start
of a new kind of day.
And beckons our hearts
and hands to do more
for the night is behind
and the day yet before.
Eyes full of grace
and hearts full of love,
hands lifted up
now praise Him above.
Awake now creation!
Have ye no fear!
Jesus the Master,
the Savior is here!

Inspired on the same hill as "Diamonds of the Dawn"
on September 6, 2013.

## OF JOB AMD THE PRODIGAL SON

Am I the righteous Job
or the son who ran away?
Who will be my judge
and who can truly say?
I only recollect
my best and noble deeds
while others see the thorns
grown from ill-cast seeds.
Job bore pain and anguish
and undeserved blame.
He could speak with God
and I desire the same.
Is that something I deserve?
So many would say, "No!"
for they recall my sins
today and long ago.
And yet the Father celebrates
whene'er a lost one's found
for the blessings of the Spirit
both marvel and abound.
And in what seems contradiction
I am prodigal and Job.
I am Joseph and his brothers
who stole his bloodied robe.
I am truth and liar,
valiant and afraid.
I am man the mystery
of best and worst both made.
How I can be reconciled?
I cannot comprehend
save I call on Jesus
and on His Name depend.
He takes me as I am
and cleanses me with Grace
so I may speak with God
and see Him face to face.

# THE FAVORED

I am my Father's favored
for reasons I don't know
and of earthly riches
I have naught to show.
Yet He speaks to me in dreams
that I can understand
and protects me with His angels
who answer His command.
"But, Lord! I am not worthy!"
I hear myself exclaim
yet who of us has chosen
what he or she became?
He put in me the willingness
to pause and hear His breath
and write so people hear it
well beyond my death.
He offered me a gift
which joyfully I took
and did not look back wistfully
at others I forsook.
He gives me ears to hear
and eyes with which to see
for insight is a gift that flows
beyond ability.
The words like manna fall
directly on the page
and so He speaks through me
to another age.
Think ye not that I am free
of debt or ill or stress
and thus the greater joy of heart
for the one gift I possess.
I look for an ending
and see not a one in sight
blinded as I am for all
but His eternal light.

# OUTRUNNING PETER

Together with Peter
I stepped out the door
and through the streets of the city
so quickly we tore.
No time for our sandals!
It was bare feet on dirt.
We must be there – Now!
– no matter the hurt.
I knew the way well,
took a shortcut or two
and stayed off the grass
because of the dew.
Then! There was the tomb
on the side of the hill!
Stone thrust aside!
The air damp and still.
All out of breath
I stopped at the door.
Why were his garments
laid soft on the floor?
My brain joined my lungs
in torment and pain.
Will nothing of Jesus
be allowed to remain?
Then up waddled Peter.
The man is so slow!
But right into the tomb!
He just had to know.
The leader before,
a follower now,
I stepped in behind him
and asked, "What, Peter? How?"
And Peter then quickly
taking the lead
said, "This is so different!
We'd better take heed.
All that has happened
has said to me, 'Grieve,'

but now there is hope
and I choose to believe.
Listen in ways
you haven't before.
I have a feeling we'll see –
Oh! – so much more!"
And Peter was right
as with courage he saw
for which Jesus so loved him
and forgave every flaw.
And He loves me too
who paused at the gate
– invited me in! –
though I thought 'twas too late.
And taking a breath
I stepped up and stepped out
yielding no longer
to fear or to doubt
and discovered a place
that shines like the dawn.

It is called Faith
and that's where I've gone.

Inspired by the Easter morning message
on March 27, 2016.

# SHADOWS ON CLOUDS

Shadows on clouds
and cold winter rain,
life often seems
like pain upon pain.
A dark narrow tunnel
with no light at the end,
a heart that's so broken
there's naught that can mend –
I see tomorrow
grim like today,
like shadows on clouds,
the black upon gray.
How can I change
this vision I see?
The biggest of changes
must happen in me.
For shadows on clouds
are made by the sun
and there is still time
before day is done
to look past the clouds
to blue sky above
and rest in the knowledge
I'm safe in God's love.

# THE ODDEST OF PLACES

I can see God
in the oddest of places,
in the sunlight on dew
and my family's faces,
in the petals of flowers
and a hummingbird's wings
for God is alive
in each of these things.
He's alive in the image
I see in the mirror.
Right here beside me?
No!  He is much nearer!
He's alive in my heart,
my mind and my hand
and in both of my feet
wherever I stand.
And when I don't see Him
I don't find it odd
for I could be blind
and still know it is God.

Written in May 2005. I don't recall
if I was in an odd or an ordinary place.

# THE HANDS OF GOD

I saw the Hands of God
reach across the sky
so powerful and huge!
And it made me wonder why
so many people
are left grieving, starving, sick,
and I thought the Hands of God
should be a bit more quick.
And as I wrote these words
I noticed my own hands,
quick to meet my needs
but slow to His commands.
And if I moved this pair of hands
with a nimbleness they've lacked
I wonder if I'd also see
God's Hands on earth to act.
Must I wait until I see
or act until I do?
To see His Hands in action
mine must be working, too.

Inspired by a cloud formation on March 14, 2010.

# AS MUCH AS

As much as ships at sea
seek a lighthouse through the gray
so we search for love
whene're we kneel to pray.
As much as tiny seeds
burst out after rain,
so my life's renewed
for Jesus takes my pain.
As much as stars and moon
add beauty to the night,
so I'll train myself
to be holy in His sight.
As much as soaring eagles
depend on warm air's rise,
so I'll spread my wings
and He'll lift me to the skies.
As much as Jesus loves me
to die upon the cross,
so I'll give my life away
and count it gain, not loss.
As much as God has blessed me
just these things He asks I do:
Fill my life with Jesus' love
and pass it on to you.

## A BACKWARDS TRADE

Man has put the tower
of Babel back together.
His effort to be God
was always "when" not "whether".
For languages have merged
with scientific ease
and hence the day has come
when all do as they please.
Oh! The wonders he has wrought
since now capacity
has finally matched the measure
of man's audacity!
Yet in the learning how
such marvels can be made
he has forgotten why
and that's a backwards trade.
For man has common tongue
in vanity and greed,
across the world and ages
still his utmost creed
and also sure the language
that always fells the tower
inevitable again
and in this very hour.

# THE WARNING

In a dream God warned me.
"A flood is on the way!"
And so I seek discernment
as I kneel and pray.
I cannot stop the waters
for I am just a man
but God has placed me here
to do the things I can.
I can be a testament
to all that's good and true
through the words I say
and all the deeds I do.
Put them all together
as planks to build an ark
and ask safety for my family
when the skies turn dark.
I can't stop the flood
and I can't stay the rain
but the miracles of God
turn losses into gain.
Let His Spirit light on me
gently as a dove.
The only cure for this sad earth
is His boundless love.

# CATHEDRALS

Some that took a thousand years
since the laying of one brick,
some are strong like fortresses
with walls both firm and thick.
Beautiful with glass
coloring the light,
every one's a miracle
designed to raise the sight.
I can hear the bells
as they call for miles around
taking thoughts to heaven
every time they sound.
And as I wander in the park
a little bit away
I find my own cathedral
and so I pause to pray.
For here the birds are chirping
above the background noise
reminding me that now's the time
to celebrate life's joys.
I gladly share the planet
with all the human race
and for a moment here with God
for He has slowed the pace.
All is fast and furious
outside cathedral walls
save for in my heart
for here is where God calls.
And for all the buildings beautiful
which man has built by hand
the heart is where my God lives
as I now understand.

# COMFORT

Comfort is the words of friendly understanding,
wisdom and advice that guide without demanding.

Comfort is a solemn bond wrapped up in a smile
that makes the warring world seem peaceful for a while.

Comfort is that moment when the sun breaks through the mist,
the startling revelation that good and light exist.

Comfort is the sharing of wisdom gloriously gained
through trust and inspiration that cannot be explained.

Comfort is the Spirit who brought these gifts to me,
who opened up my heart and two blind eyes to see.

Comfort is a blanket on a cold and wintry day,
warmth that gives my mind a chance to fly away.

Comfort is a cup of coffee in my waking hands
and taking time to drink it in spite of life's demands.

Comfort is a fire to warm and make the spirit bright
that promises serenity all throughout the night.

Comfort is the notion that things misunderstood
can with contemplation turn out as they should.

Comfort is my body and spirit joined as one
when in my search for enmity I for once saw none.

# DEEP AS THE OCEAN

My sin is as deep as the ocean.
I'm buried by mountainous waves.
With no breath to call I but think
And instantly Lord Jesus saves!
For His love reaches higher than mountains
That reach beyond clouds in the sky.
I marvel and wonder at Jesus
Who died to save those such as I.
His forgiveness is like the vast heavens
And fuller than clear summer night
And more than the dawn does the morning
He fills my heart full of His light.
His power is greater than tempests
That raise those great waves of the sea.
With a lift of His finger they calm
And Jesus does all this for me!
And what in thanks can I give Him
Who loves, forgives and reigns?
Only my heart to make pure
And from the prison of sin, my chains!
For deep as the ocean He reaches!
The skies and the heavens are His.
One with the Father and Spirit
Before time's beginning, He is.

# CHARIOTS AND HORSES

Chariots and horses,
powers and forces,
so mighty each in their day,
made from the dust
like all things they must
return once more to the clay.
Arrows and bows
and catapult throws
once feared now rot in the field,
the king of these stones
now nothing but bones
that lie broken beneath his own shield.
For nothing can hide
from time's ruthless tide
nor one more moment ever cajole.
With an outcome so bleak
where does a man seek
a home for his permanent soul?
Not from wars or from nations
but from his relations
with Christ the Savior and King
and no chariot or horse
can throw me off course
when it is to His robe that I cling!

# LAST CALL OF THE BUGLER

Soft short notes
the splendors of breath
that hold for a moment
the advent of death,
and somehow the melody
hangs on the breeze
while the lips and the lungs
that played it with ease
struggle against
their weakness of form
wherein beats a heart
gentle and warm.
Soft, short and sweet
yet courageous and brave,
these are testament tones
to the love that he gave.
The last note is longer
and as I strain so to hear
thousands of stars
in the sunset appear.
Each light is a life
the music has found
- The bugler reborn! -
for each raises the sound
of the triumph
of the spirit of man
living forever
as no body yet can.
Listen with me
to the bugler's last call;
raise yours to your lips
as he lets his fall.

# WHEN YOU KNOW

I had a dream this morning.
God had written down my name.
My present and my future
were not at all the same.
All the information
that He had passed to me
were writ in many languages
and to the world set free.
People I would meet,
I saw their names in gold.
Everything that's happening
has ever been foretold.
What do I do with knowledge
that has been so imparted?
I share it near and far
for the action's long since started.
Lift the wands of peace and love
and part the sea of woe.
Plant the trees of love and life;
nurture, watch them grow.
You can make a change
if you believe it so
but the future really alters
when it's something that you know.

"Last Call of the Bugler" was written for my brother, Gene.
My book, **The Toy Bugle,** is dedicated to him.
He was the bugler in our Scout troop.

# INTO THE LION'S EYES

I have looked into the lion's eyes.
Ferociously they shine!
Like the wounded antelope
I hear them say, "You're mine!"
There is a place beyond, below
the conscious mind so deep,
one that only lion's eyes
can waken from its sleep.
"Live!" it cries. "Survive!"
"Rise up from your pain!"
My heart beats wildly now
yet frozen, I remain.
I hear the lion roar
as it saunters towards the kill
and there is but one option:
to conquer fear with will!
And though my side is bleeding
I quickly leap away
before the lion's eyes
can claim me as their prey.
I am stronger now
and wiser for my foe
and for the hidden parts of me
that I have come to know.
I escaped the lion's eyes
and I no longer doubt
the strength of spirit deep within
nor the greater One without.

# DON'T FEED THE SEAGULLS

"You can't feed the seagulls here!
It says so on that sign.
If you do you'll have to pay
'cause there's a hundred dollar fine."
But the seagulls must not have read those words
and hungry they must be
for them to take a cracker
from a lawbreaker like me.
As I hold each cracker high
the seagulls gather to be fed.
How many people hunger
for what nourishes much more than bread?
"Do not feed the seagulls
in China or Bangladesh
for we're afraid what will happen here
if they taste what's good and fresh."
But yes, I will feed the seagulls
on this or any beach
and I will spread the Gospel!
There's a whole wide world to reach.

I wrote "Don't Feed the Seagulls" on September 6, 2002
for brave friends who ventured overseas as missionaries.

# NO SHELTER IN BETHLEHEM

The air's so cold!  The wind's so brisk,
no shelter in Bethlehem tonight,
a mother's tears His only warmth
until the morning light.
I would have been in Bethlehem
to greet and welcome You
but I missed the signs the angels gave
and only shepherds knew.
I would have given a place to sleep
and songs before a fire.
Instead You faced the cold alone
with only donkeys as a choir.
I would have given blankets
to protect You from the wind
but I didn't see You coming
and on me You could not depend.
Lord, how can You still love me?
I've failed time and time again.
I missed the chance to celebrate
for where my hands and heart have been.

The lightning strikes!  The thunder rolls!
It storms in Jerusalem tonight.
There's warmth in the blood of Jesus
as His followers take flight.
I would have spoken up for You
but I was afraid to die.
I said I'd protect You Lord
but I didn't even try.
I would have said I know You
but my fears got the best of me.
I said I'd stay with You till the end
but I took the chance to flee.
I would have believed You'd rise again
but they put You in the grave.
What made You want to die for me
for who was I to save?

Lord, I do not understand
but I know Your love's so great.
Can You take me with You now?
Please say it's not too late.

The air so fresh, the sea so blue,
there's life in Galilee tonight.
There's warmth in my heart to welcome Him
and finally set things right.
I have come to Galilee
to listen to my Saviour speak.
I heard it from the shepherds
and now I salvation seek.
I have bread to offer Him
and with you I'll gladly share
for I have seen the miracles
and felt His loving care.
I have words to speak for Him
and hands to do good deeds.
I have feet to follow Him
any place He leads.
Lord, I feel Your love for me
and return that love I do.
I will live so that those who watch
in seeing me, see only You.

# CLIMB THE RED MOUNTAIN

Only for an instant
late in the waning year,
only one place to see it
and I am standing here.
The leaves have turned from green
to orange, yellow, and brown,
and are red only on the mountain
just as the sun goes down.
Beautiful beyond belief,
I am the only one who sees it!
This chance may come but a single time;
I must act now to seize it!
Climb the crimson mountain slopes
as the sun sinks low in the sky!
What will you find when you reach the top?
You won't know unless you try!

*Climb the Red Mountain* was my second book of poems.
I wrote the poem in November of 2002.

# MAY YOUR LIPS ALWAYS BE LONG ENOUGH

May your lips always be long enough
to kiss the ones you love.
May your skies always be bright enough
to lift your eyes above.
May your hands always be strong enough
to hold on to what's good
yet wise enough to let things go
when your heart says that you should.
May your feet always be sure enough
to find the narrow way
and kind enough to those you love
to bring you home someday.
May your heart always have courage
enough to carry on
when hands and feet have failed
and all your strength is gone.
May your spirit then be bold enough
to look to that bright sky
and fill your soul with faith enough
to give you wings to fly!

I sign my children's book *I Don't Want to Kiss a Llama!*
with the first two lines of this poem.

## FOOTSTEPS IN THE GARDEN

A shuffled foot, an easy laugh,
there are footsteps in the garden
to celebrate last week's parade,
the one that Jesus starred in.
Softly now we speak
and talk of what's to be:
Peace on earth for everyone,
a certain victory.
So sure we are that all is well
we soon fall fast asleep
but there is one who carries on,
His promises to keep.
Would that we had heeded Him
when He gave us call,
Jesus, God's only Son,
who lived to save us all.
A footstep in the garden,
a sandal on a stone,
Jesus, the one and only
now stands guard alone.

A snapping stick, an angry shout,
there are footsteps in the garden.
Even blessed with Jesus' love
how human hearts can harden!
Fiercely now the voices raise
and with them rock and fist.
"This man is not as one of us!
Do not allow Him to exist!"
In an instant all is lost!
My Master's gone away
and I cannot ever save Him now
no matter what I pray.
The crowds that cheered now mock Him
and the blood runs in His eyes.
Alone now on a cross of wood
my Lord Jesus dies.
No footsteps in the garden,

just a bloody stone,
for the Son of God was made like me
of human flesh and bone.


"Hosanna in the Highest!"
There are footsteps in the garden!
Rejoice now one and all
for Jesus has won pardon.
Hear the angels singing
and join their happy chorus!
Jesus died and rose again
and He did it all for us!
Who has eyes to see?
Who has ears to hear?
Jesus has defeated death
and there's nothing left to fear.
Yes, I will heed Him now
for I have a second chance.
What He's offered me is yours as well
so join me in the dance!
Joyous footsteps in the garden
and happy, dancing feet
to celebrate Christ's holy gift
and victory complete!

## THE SOUND OF FREEDOM'S SAIL

I hear her in the cheering crowds
as she marks the Fourth of July
even with the fireworks
exploding in the sky.
Above the roar of crashing waves
in the stiffest ocean gale,
snapping in the wind,
she is freedom's billowed sail.
With open eyes I look to her,
the red, the white and blue,
yet even in the darkest night
her sounds keep coming through,
calling loudly, "One and all,
never be afraid!
March beside the Stars and Stripes
in freedom's grand parade!"

With sounds of battle crashing
and the din of falling shells,
through her torn and tattered weeping
her agony she tells.
She cries for all her children,
the noble and the brave,
who knew the cost of freedom
yet for us all, they gave.
With moistened eyes I'm blinded
but I can hear her still
standing guard for those who lie
beneath this sacred hill,
calling softly, "Everyone!
Remember each brave soul.
To live in peace and freedom
should also be your goal."

I hear her every morning
above the trumpet call
in the softly rustling breeze
that touches one and all.
And she calls me in the evening
as the sun begins to set.
Though taken down and folded
she's not through talking yet.
I close my eyes and touch her
and hold her to my chest.
Of all the flags I've ever held
this one is the best,
whispering to me, "All is well.
You are safe with me.
When you hear me calling in the wind,
take heart! For you are free!"

On February 15, 2003 I heard a flag suddenly flap
in the breeze as I walked on the hill near my home.
This is what it said to me.

## THE WIND IN FREEDOM'S SAIL

I hear that sail a-rippling
as with the wind it fills.
To navigate these narrow straits
takes all our strength and skills.
In such waters we are tempted
to fly a lesser sail
but freedom is the answer
and with her we will prevail.
She billows full with stories
of dangers bravely met
in stronger storms than those we face.
No! We shall not forget!
Reminding me, "Remember!
This sail's sewn not with seams
but with the blood of patriots
and their undying dreams!"

I hear that sail a-tearing
as the angry storm draws nigh
and wonder what the future holds
as I look through her to the sky.
What can hold together
the fabric this storm parts?
The honor and the faith
that live in human hearts!
I hear her, our mended sail,
whom the sudden gust has fed.
"God has set the course for us
in all He's done and said,
telling me, 'America!
Do not your God deny.
Always seek the wind of truth
and you will never die!'"

I hear that sail a-flutter
as we both set out to sea
and wonder whence it comes,
this wind that sets us free.
I hear it in the voices
of generations past,
"It is the breath of God
that drives our ship so fast."

A sail that reaches outward
from this, our blessed land,
guided by the faith
that we are in His hand,
singing to me, "Praise the Lord!
He blesses and He gives.
He is the wind in freedom's sail
and with His touch, she lives!"

This poem is companion and completion
to the previous one. It was written
on November 22, 2003.

## AMERICA IS

America is baseball
on a hot summer's day.
It's fireworks at the grandstand
when the band begins to play,
family picnics in the park,
taking children to the zoo,
the freedom to do the work you love
and to love the work you do.
Americans are people
who hold their families dear
and all of us will rally round
when our neighbor's call we hear.
America blessed with bounty,
America the land we love,
our liberty's a legacy
from the hand of God above.

America is patriots' dreams
as they cross the Delaware.
It's engineers and astronauts
as into space we dare.
It's soldiers who defend our homes
here or across the sea,
citizens who cast their votes
so thoughts and words stay free.
Americans are people
who hold their heroes high.
We're heroes one and all
when we answer freedom's holy cry.
America home to heroes,
America the land we love,
our liberty's a legacy
from the hand of God above.

America is God's blessed land,
a people to be born,
born in freedom to celebrate
and blow the victory horn.
America is God's gift to us,
indeed to all the earth,
for Americans know freedom
and they know what freedom's worth.
Americans are people
who on Almighty God depend.
When we look to Him
our land He will defend.
America full of faith,
America the land we love,
our liberty's a legacy
from the hand of God above.

This is one of my first poems.
I wrote "America Is" in July of 2002.

# OUR EAGLE

He's been stretching wings
since the day he first breathed air
and every time he conquered one
he'd find another dare.
One more challenge to pursue
and chase it to the end,
his fierce determination,
on that we could depend.
And now those wings are ready!
Our son is fully grown.
He has felt his freedom now
and to such heights he's flown.
And on this day and from this place
his journey starts anew
and though we can't go with him
the path he chose is true.
Honor, courage, faith,
he carries these things high.
Our son flies as an eagle!
There are no limits in his sky.
And so we proudly watch
as he rises on those wings,
praising God and praying for
all the blessings His love brings.

Inspired by our son, Ryan, an Eagle Scout.

## THE GIFT OF JESUS' SMILE

Is it just a dream,
the kind things being said?
I thought that as a poet
they'd wait 'til I was dead.
They'd wait to buy a book
but today I sold so many!
Wasn't it just yesterday
I didn't have a penny?
And yet it isn't selling books
that brings me greatest joy.
I love to hear the laughter
of every girl and boy.
A thousand happy faces!
(I count their families, too.)
I have changed the world
with this thing I do.
And thanks to those who love me
and believed without despair
I have reached the Promised Land
and built a mansion there.
Everyone can visit.
Sit and stay a while!
Thank you, God, for giving us
the gift of Jesus' smile.

Beginning in 2006 I have been blessed
to recite my children's poems  at Grant's Farm in St. Louis.
This poem reminds me how fortunate I am.

# THE LIGHT I LET IN

Such a dark and dreary day
I cannot recall.
Here inside my somber room
I can barely see at all.
And I wonder what I've done
that I should be forsaken.
If God has put the lights out
why should I awaken?
And yet I hear the sound
of my alarm clock ringing.
I quickly turn it off
but every bird is singing!
I struggle to the window.
What kind of day is this?
I find behind the curtain
the day I'd picked to miss.
It's ripe with colors chosen
for my own eyes alone
that had I stayed in bed
I would have never known.
I recognize God's glory
in this day I now begin
and realize that my view depends
on the light that I let in.

Written May 3, 2005. It was a Tuesday.

## THE COMMON TRIBULATIONS

We are not above
the common tribulations
that confront, confuse
and trouble our relations.
Often it's the little things
that start with just a trickle
yet add up to remind us
how life can be so fickle.
High atop the mountain
and in the moment next
frustrated, angry
and, most of all, perplexed
at how the tumble happened
– Oh! – so quickly
and life that seemed so smooth
has become quite prickly.
For no matter how you think
life has made you wise
the common tribulations
will catch you by surprise.
And then it's time to take
a step back from the fray,
reflect and reevaluate
and go about your day
taking with you confidence
that you are in God's hands
and that for Jesus' sacrifice
He surely understands.

## TO GIVE AGAIN

Oh, to have the courage
to never count the cost
of unsuccessful ventures
and precious treasures lost
but instead to look ahead
when the daylight's gone
through the night to the light
of tomorrow's dawn.
And in the treasure of the time
God has granted all
gain the gift of spirit
whatever outcomes fall.
Then to learn that having
is only for a day
and that to keep forever
we must first give away .
But how the pain of losing
such bitterness imparts!
To give again when all is lost
opens up our hearts.
To try and fail and try again
is a test of strength and will
and to remember and to give again –
is that not greater still?

# OUT OF ABUNDANCE

Out of abundance
a table is set
for today is a day
for joy not regret.
Gather the food
so all may be fed
and see that there's love
served with the bread.
For where there's abundance
hunger shall wane
so give away all
and let none remain.
Let everyone come
to share in the feast
for I imagine today
that I am the least
and the poorest
to stand in the line.
Will anyone dare
switch their place with mine?
I'm afraid that my needs
will all be ignored
but then I see Jesus
who's ambling toward
and followed by thousands
once poor like me
whom Jesus has fed
and by love set free.
For out of abundance
of love and of grace
Jesus has offered
and given His place.

## THOMAS DOWDEN

It was on an application
the lad reversed his name
and realized that in his mind
and heart he felt the same.
"I need proof," he thought.
"If I trust, you might just lie.
How is it He could rise again?
It's over when you die.
He'll have to hold His hands out
for me to touch and see."
And so began the journey
of doubtin' Thomas D.

His mother made him go to church
but he couldn't hide his sneers.
When his sister sang in children's choir
he covered both his ears.
They all went to Grandma's house
each Thanksgiving Day
and she surprised her grandson
when she asked Thomas to pray.
"Grandma, I don't think that Jesus
wants to hear a prayer from me
'cause if He's real He knows my heart
and I'm doubtin' Thomas D."

His grandma cocked her head
and peered into his eyes.
"Thomas," she said, "You're at that age
and this is no surprise.
There are things that you're unsure of
and we must have a talk
so humor an old woman
and join me for a walk.
Dear Thomas, I think that Jesus
and I would both agree.
Now's the time to speak your heart
'cause I'm certain Granny D.!"

They talked of many things, these two,
the child she lost at birth,
the sorrow that she felt the day
they put his grandpa in the earth.
Yet it wasn't sadness that he saw in her
for her face was bright with joy
and as the Spirit filled her up
she reached out and touched the boy.
'Twas Jesus' hands he felt and saw
and he fell down to his knees
and there the Spirit changed his doubts
into certainties.

Jesus knows your heart and mind
but the choice is up to you
so when the clouds of doubt swirl round
what are you going to do?
Will you try to hide it
and store it up inside?
For it is an ancient struggle
'tween His love, your pride.
Will it take a vision
to finally set you free?
Then look into the face of love
like doubtin' Thomas D.

Remembering Ernest Frederick Taylor.

## QUICKLY FOR QUICKLY

When trials were tough
and answers were few
in spite of myself
that's when I grew.
And losing one time
meant winning the next
for life does not follow
a writ-in-stone text.
I made my choices
and make more today.
You do the same
and find your own way.
It might break your heart
to be chasing a star
but do it you must
to know who you are.
Oh! How I wish
that by clearing the field
those answers you seek
could be quickly revealed.
But all I can do
is to say with a sigh
that I've done my best
and it's your turn to try.
I wish there were more
I could say that I've learned
but the deepest of wisdom
has to be earned.
When you seek wisdom
you'll find tribulation
for it is through trial
there comes revelation.
Yet when other men fail
you will stand tall

and see for a moment
over the wall.
Remember that moment
and share it in word –
Quickly! – for quickly
wisdom is blurred.
So just for an instant
e'er it passes from sight
share what you see
of God's truth and light!

A quick dunk of my head underwater in our hot tub
inspired "In the Sudden Silence" on November 22, 2003.
And I wrote it as soon as I dried off!

## THE REDIRECT

I paused
beside the path
to say a little prayer
and wondered
at events
which conspired
to bring me there.
For I desired a different goal
than the one
that lay ahead
and wondered why the Lord
sent me out this way
instead.
And in our conversation
I came to understand
than any prayer
I utter
does not move
His Hand.
It simply redirects me
on the path
that He has set
for the treasure's
in the traveling!
That's the gift we get.
And the closer that I stay
the more I realize
that walking hand-in-hand
with Him
is by far
the greatest prize.

I wrote "The Redirect" and "The Gift of Jesus' Smile"
on my mother's birthday in different years.

# FINDING PEACE

People carry signs,
give speeches, shout and chant,
but when it comes to bringing peace
it seems that these things can't.
Yet still they make the papers
and statesmen meet and talk
almost to the dotted line
when both sides decide to balk.
And what things do I do
to bring peace throughout the land?
I listen for the voice of God
to help me understand.
And then I sit and write
the words that start to flow
revealing truths to me
that I would never know:
"Peace is such a fragile thing,
broken by the breeze,
found by those who seek it
when they ask God on their knees."
So I won't be seeking headlines
as so many people do
but praying quietly for peace
because – I want some, too.

Inspired by my sister, Carol.

# WHAT I LEARNED

There's a part of my old brain
that tries to take me back
to school or work or circumstance
when I faced undue attack.
I felt it in my dreams last night
and it created this concern.
What, from all my life and trials,
did I really learn?
I'm still confused and caught
by rules and regulations
causing me the same exact
rants and consternations.
I can't tell if someone else
is genuine or fake.
If one life is not enough for that,
how many will it take?
There is still decided lack
in my bank account
and in my time remaining
I'll use that whole amount.
Yet I see the sense of wonder,
excitement and surprise
in the expressions of the children
and reflected in their eyes.
Maybe this is what He meant
when Jesus spoke and said
to enter heaven one must be
as a child is led.
Shake off all the trappings
that you thought protected
and look into the Savior's eyes.
Now you are connected!
For at the end illusion
dims and slowly fades.
Here is where one walks with God
in green and pastured glades
and there to see a vision
unlike those of earth,
God's eternal glory
at your spirit's birth.

# WINGS ON FEET OF CLAY

Wings on feet of clay,
I ponder on the phrase.
Are there ways my spirit
can this body raise?
Wing-ed feet run faster
and touch not earth but air.
Thoughts on wings can take me
almost anywhere.
Thoughts on wings on feet of clay,
body, spirit, mind—
Earth's my home, the special place
where all of these combined.
Will my spirit linger
when my body's done
or is it on a journey
that has just begun?
Where and whither will it go
freed from feet of clay?
Deep into the dawning
of a brand-new day!
It will not look back
at its broken shell
but rather seek the highest place
and therein will it dwell.
I am not the wings or feet
but the combination
special and unique
in all of God's creation.
I am the two as one
tethered for a time,
a place the spirit grows
so it may reach its prime.
A spirit is a pair of wings
finally on its own
yet joining with a flock alike
it is not alone.
Can you hear them calling?
They circle close for me,
a pair of wings from feet of clay
finally set free.

# ASK THE LITTLE CHILDREN

I ask the little children
to gather at my knee
for from there the light of heaven
is easier to see.
No one understands
lest as a child he sees
and trusts in me as much
as does one of these.

They tell the children not
to dare to trouble me
but lest they ask who of them
will find themselves set free?
No one finds the kingdom
save I show the way
so trust me like those children
who bow their heads to pray.

I like to watch the children
with faces all aglow
who for youth and innocence
know the one thing all must know.
Kindliness and goodness
come from God above
and when we look to Jesus
we see the face of love.

Can it be so simple?
Are there no laws to learn?
Only this: Salvation
is not a thing to earn.
Accept it as a gift
in wonder and in awe
and enter heaven as a child
with neither stain nor flaw.

Precious gifts from Thee to me
are these!  All praises be!
The lame can walk.
The mute can talk
and the blind can finally see.
Blessings unfold from Thee, my Lord,
and I pray on bended knee
that the world beholds the wondrous gift
that flowed from Galilee:
The sacrifice of Jesus Christ
who died to set us free.

My mother Marjorie and I wrote this poem together
in November of 2016. It was fun!

# ASHES FROM THE FIRE

The time has come.
They've called my name.
It's time for me to go
And I'm the one
Who has conspired
That this should all be so.
For years I blamed
Someone else,
Anyone but me,
But now at last
At the end
It's my own guilt I see.
Salvation is
Impossible
Through any strength of mine.
I ask God
For miracles
E'er I to death resign.
There is no answer
From the skies
No angels from above
And I accept
I don't deserve
At all my Master's love.
How it must
Have hurt that day
Upon that awful tree
When Jesus died
For all my sins
There on Calvary.
He cried out
In pain and fear
And yet no answer came
And it is with
A different tune
I now invoke His name.
Not for earthly blessings
He's given

And I've squandered
Nor to solve life's mysteries
That for so long
I've pondered.
For this one thing alone,
"Lord, take away my sin!
Let me fellowship with You
As brother once again!"
For that is what He promised
When He rose up
From the dead
Not for
Worldly treasures
I have pursued instead.
Ashes from the fire
All these things shall be
But the treasure
My Lord died to save
I know at last
Was me.

# THE TREE OF THE POWER TO CONTAIN GOOD AND EVIL

For years they lived in the garden
and often ate fruit from this tree
so Adam and Eve passed on to all
who followed this ability.
To contain is to have and to hold
and for safety to keep locked away
but so many have opened that box
from the state of the world seen today.
There is evil contained in revenge
and evil in words harshly used
and evil when people do nothing
when others are badly abused.
But out of the very same hand
that in anger a clenched fist is raised
comes a gift of good so abundant
that all who see are amazed.
And wouldn't it be nice if we watchers
and hypocrites see not only the bad
but the good contained in our fellows
and instead of angry be glad?
For all of us have this great power
to contain both evil and good
and shouldn't there be celebration
when one of us acts as he should?
We had this power before
Adam and Eve did partake
the fruit of the tree of the knowledge
and became aware of the choices we make.
All who are good contain evil
and not every thought can be pure.
Evil contained is still evil.
Oh God!  Give me strength to endure!
I have the power and knowledge.
I contain the right and the wrong.
You alone know the battles I waged
and the struggles I faced hard and long.
I contain good and evil
as man has done and will do

for God alone is just good
and thus His word only is true.
I give Him all evil thoughts
that are contained in my heart and my head
and the good I offer but He
says give this to others instead.
For there is evil enough
in the world in its present state.
Release the good you contain
and find its power also is great.
Everyone knows I have evil
which I'll contain 'til the day that I die
but that doesn't mean that the good
I tried to do is a lie.

# A POEM BY THE RAIN

This poem has been written
by the drizzling rain
which from my work has caused me
for a moment to refrain.
It is indeed a slower pace
than I am used to running
and I find I do not need
my usual grace and cunning.
A poem by the rain
has unexpectedly
brought thoughts and observations
from deep inside of me.
For it is in the stillness
and the quiet calm
that I can feel God's Spirit
flowing through His palm.
It touches me in manners
that I commonly don't feel
for poems made by nature
are remarkable and real.
When I lack the words
God gives me what to say.
The poem by the rain
taught me that today.

I wrote this poem at Grant's Farm
on September 18, 2011.

# AN ACT OF TRUE KINDNESS

An act of true kindness
is an incredible sight
for taking the wrong
and making it right.
Give someone who's hungry
a piece of your bread
and you'll find that your spirit
also is fed.
Give someone who's weak
a strong hand to hold
and look for the same
should you dare to grow old.
Some people need time.
Try spending a while
sharing a story,
a laugh or a smile.
Kindness is never
one way like a street.
Without it no person
is ever complete.
Isn't there someone
you can help out today?
There is if you'll take
this moment to pray.
Reach out with your thoughts,
your heart and your mind
to try to bring forward
those left far behind.
Try it today
as never before
then go out tomorrow
and do even more.

# THE UNDERSTANDING

It started with a prayer.
Good things always do
and yet it takes an effort
to make such dreams come true.
But effort by itself
though it may bring you far
will not take you closer
than a mountain to a star.
There is not enough of strength
or valor in a man
lest he rely upon the One
with Whose help he can.
Life demands the courage
to dream and do and dare
and the understanding
to start and end with prayer.

My wife Sharon was praying for me before we even met.
And she still does. . .

## PETER IS DROWNING

"Peter is drowning!
The man is a fool!
Stay in the boat!
That's the number one rule!
But no! He had to show off
his faith like a boast!
Walking on water?
I'd stay close to the coast!
But he's reaching for Jesus
and no one else is.
Maybe the problem
is mine and not his.
What kind of example
has Jesus been setting?
Be brave for your faith!
We all were forgetting.
And Peter reminded
at expense to himself.
Maybe it's time
to get mine off the shelf
and to start working
for the kingdom of love
and counting on miracles
sent from above."

# I NEVER KNEW

I speak in tongues
I never knew,
am amazed at pictures
I just drew:
The evening sun,
the morning dew,
evidence
of my God Who
proves His Word
is ever true
searching, seeking,
all for you.
These to touch
the heart and soul,
a tiny part
of God's great whole
and yet to me
they're everything.
From deep within
they quickly spring
to wash away
my daily cares.
Such gifts He grants
to he who dares
admit, accept
and then proclaim
salvation in
Lord Jesus' name.

# A FEATHER FROM AN ANGEL'S WING

It weighs no more than a spider's web
damp in the morning dew,
a feather from an angel's wing
that offers but one clue
as to the nature of God's love
and nurture of the soul
for this feather from an angel's wing
signifies my role:
To quiet soft the noises
and voices gathered round
so all who listen may someday
hear one special sound.
The rustle of ten thousand
angels taking wing,
one must attend so carefully
to notice such a thing!
For angel wings are silent
more than softest breeze
yet once it has been heard
it's recognized with ease
and sought as is the notion
that God blesses those who dare
as all who seek Him with their heart
discover Him right there.

# THE COMFORTER COMES

The Comforter comes
When we ask
Not because we've
Done some task.
Prayer is not
A magic wand
To which the heavens
Must respond.
But it is simply
A seeking out
In times of certainty
And, yes, of doubt,
A call that says,
"I need a friend"
Or "Help me see
Around the bend."
The Comforter is
Always near
But those are words
He likes to hear.
"I will send Him,"
Jesus said
But we all try
So hard instead.
Gotta do it
On our own
Yet wonder if
We had known
How close our friend
Has always been
If we could do it
All again
We would ask Him,
"Come along!"
"Help us turn
To right the wrong!"
"We are weak!
Make us strong!"

"Fill us with
Your joyous song."
And as I write
Suddenly
An idea
Comes to me:
These are things
He's always done
Though I may
Have lost or won.
The prayer makes not
His choice of going
But simply is
A way of knowing.
Helpful to
My heart because
I know now all
The things He does.
He's my strength
When I am weak.
He helps me choose
Which goals to seek.
Control me- No!
Help me - Yes!
For prayer is certainty
Not guess
And knowledge helps
A person bear
The weight of earthly
Toil and care.
I'm stronger for
My simple prayer
Just because
I know He's there.

## THE ONE BLUE FIREFLY

My quiet summer evening
was interrupted by her cry.
"Daddy! Come and look!" my daughter said.
"It's blue! That firefly."
I blinked. "I think I missed it.
Honey, was it really blue?
Should I take you to the doctor?
Are your eyes tricking you?"
"Daddy, please believe me," she pleaded.
"You can see it if you try!
Wouldn't it be something
to see just one blue firefly?"
Reluctantly I nodded
and followed where she pranced
as on and off above the field
the fireflies flew and danced.
Yellow, yellow, yellow, yellow.
Not a blue one to be found.
Is my mind so set
that even eyes are bound?
Then, suddenly! I see it
like a touch of azure sky!
What other things are possible
if there's one blue firefly?
Perhaps it's not believing,
just opening my mind,
for if I can see this firefly
who knows what else I'll find?
So keep your eyes wide open
for that one blue firefly
and the other little miracles
God sends you by and by.

# CAUGHT IN THE CURRENT

Pale green pastures
and deep blue skies
mean spring's come again.
Oh, how the time flies!
The young man I was
is now forty-nine.
These grownups I see
were once children of mine.
The trees are all budding.
The flowers are next
and some of the animals
seems quite perplexed
as I always am
at the beginning of spring.
Why must I question
such a beautiful thing?
It seems like enough
to live for today
and give thanks for the moment
in my own special way.
So I'll say a prayer
and walk through the grasses
caught in the current
of time as it passes.

"The One Blue Firefly" was inspired by our daughter Erin
and by the blue firefly on July 9, 2004  in Byrnes Mill,
Missouri. "Caught in the Current" was written in 2006.

## AS IF MEN

"Blessed are the peacemakers."
That was Jesus' phrase,
an oddity in thought back then
as in these later days.
It goes against the grain
to seek a soft solution
and we blame the ones who try
for the rise of destitution.
But blame should go where blame should go,
to the perpetrator.
The peacemaker defers
what will likely happen later.
But in that breath of time
there is that moment glorious,
a vision of an age
that dawns with peace victorious.
It is just a dream,
a day I'll never see,
but everyone who strives for it
will surely blessed be.
Parlay not with weapon
nor fear nor threat of gun,
trust and love to rule
where today there's none.
And as for me I will share
such peaceful thoughts as flow
from He who blessed the peacemakers
so many years ago.

# THOUGH GENTLE THE SEA

I don't know why but I like to build
castles in the sand
but they never do last
as long as I'd planned.
For there's always a chance
it will get hit by a wave
and then there is nothing
I can do that will save
the towers from falling
and the bridge from collapse
for even when gentle
the sea always laps
away at creations
from the mind of a man
who builds just to prove
if he wants to he can.
But the marvels of his
will be swept away
and all works will be God's
at the end of the day.
And yet here I kneel
to build castles in sand
with my feet in the sea
and the earth in my hand.

## ROSES AFTER RAIN

Roses after rain
has washed the dirt away
catch the falling sunlight
at the finish of the day.
Shadows on the petals
and drops of diamond dew
give the rose appearance
as it were fresh and new.
And with the raindrops life
has blossomed once again
and the rose pours out the love
that just keep flowing in.
Oh! To be a perfect rose
that sin could never stain!
Jesus, Lord, make me clean
like roses after rain.

Red roses are my wife Sharon's favorite flower.
And I think mine as well

# THE EAGLE'S VIEW

Level with the eagle's eye
I find a grander view
for from this lofty perch I see
His promises are true.
Long I've watched the eagle
as I stood so far below
but now I've climbed the mountain
and what I thought before, I know.
For I can see the valley
and mountain silhouette.
The journey and the lesson
are ones I won't forget.
Now even with the eagle
I feel my spirit soar.
Can it somehow be
that God gives even more?
How far, how high, how free
in this earthly body frail?
Above the eagle's eye I rise
on life's eternal trail!

I wonder if flying is fun or just ordinary for a bird.

# FROM MY TASK

I've been taken
from my task.
"Why?" I've learned
not to ask.
For I say
enough it is
to know that time
and I are His.
Here He needs me.
Now! Today.
Discernment comes
as I pray
not to question
reason, rhyme.
All is answered
in God's time.
And so I wander
aimlessly
knowing that
He's seeking me.
Confident
He will find
reassures
heart and mind.
All my tasks
whisked away
so I may be
His today.

# SEAGULLS TO THE SEA

They hover o'er the waters
on the rising wind
searching for a meal
on which their lives depend.
They tarry not in fear
of the water far below.
Indeed each one seems eager
for the chance to go.
Then suddenly one folds its wings
and starts its journey down
and I wonder, "Does it think
that it might one day drown?"
But there! It breaks the surface!
A fish wriggles in its beak
and I have learned a lesson
about this knowledge that I seek:
That to be truly nourished
I must act like this brave bird
and every day I live
dive into God's word.

We lived in Corpus Christi, Texas when Ryan and Erin were little
and our visits to Padre Island inspired this poem.

## AS A LEAF FALLS

A leaf falls from a barren tree
and elevates my sight
towards the waning crescent moon
and an eagle's rising flight.
One must rise and one must fall.
That's how things on earth must be
but I wonder if there's more
in this sight I see.
For the leaf is like the body
that grows old in just one season
and the eagle like the spirit
that soars for but one reason –
to feel the breath of God
underneath its wings
coming close to Him
with all the joy that brings.
And I pray that I may lift my wings
so God can carry me,
my spirit like an eagle
on winds to set it free.

My first book was ***Don't Feed the Seagulls***.
It was published in 2003.

# LEAVES OF THANKSGIVING

Leaves of thanksgiving
burst out from the tree
and dance in the sunlight,
such a great joy to see!
An offering of life
that this tree has grown
making no claims
that these are its own –
Here is God's answer
in the splendor of spring
that to truly give thanks
we yield everything!
And I realize in watching
that my spring is here
and I offer to God
everything I hold dear,
knowing at last
it's not mine to give
yet giving it anyway
each day that I live!

Written in Forest Park in May of 2005.
The tree that lost its leaves in the fall
grew them again in the spring.

# SURRENDERING ISAAC

"What kind of God demands
that I give up my son?
Whatever He has asked of me
I have always done.
I have left my parents, my friends,
the city where I grew.
How can this God love me
if He wants Isaac, too?"
These are questions Abraham
must've asked down deep
and the ones I asked today
for the things I want to keep.
My house, my job, my car,
the family who I treasure –
can a God who loves me
deny me every pleasure?
Yet one by one they fall
and at last I bend the knee
and at His feet I realize
what He wanted me to see.
The joy of being One with Him,
the beauty of His face,
nothing that I ever owned
could this one thing replace.
What Isaacs do you cling to
that you value more than He?
Surrender them with love and grace
and God will set you free.

## WHERE I WOULD HAVE GONE

I would have gone to Paris,
to London or to Rome
but they didn't want me there
so here I sit at home.
I would have tried Chicago
or even New York City
but I never got that far
and I'd think it was a pity
save for the quiet whispering
God puts in my ear.
"Today it is important
that you remain right here.
For there is something special
I wanted you to see
so you can help someone else
know life differently.
It might be the sunlight
on a butterfly's new wing
to tell you that the Lord of hosts
values such a thing.
It could be the smile you see
on your son's or daughter's face
to tell you that these gifts of time
are things you can't replace.
It might be a dream
you remember as you wake
to say My gifts are infinite
and there for you to take.
So calm yourself and do not fear!
Act within My will
and know that whither you may go
I am with you still."

## THE LEAST

I did not face the lions
in the stadium or den.
I did not feel the nail
as the soldiers drove it in.
I did not watch the martyrs
suffer pain and death.
While others agonized
I have been given breath.
And I do not know the reasons,
the wherefores and the whys
God gives me thoughts to write
that I do not recognize.
For they are not my own.
I did nothing to deserve
and the least that I can do
is praise my God and serve
the people who need comfort –
the lame, the blind, the ill –
and be glad to do all good things
that God declares His will!

I helped my father when he was ill
and ever since I've been blessed
with poems such as these to share.

# DROPS AFTER RAIN

I sit and I listen
to drops after rain
and it gives rise to thoughts
I strive to explain.
Those drops are the rainfall
that got caught by a tree
and with a touch of the wind
they now fall on me.
And I think of the gifts
that others once found
falling on me
like drops towards the ground.
The gifts of the Spirit
from a time that has passed
like drops after rain
have fallen at last.
The deeds of the saints
and the freedom we know
are drops after rain
that fell long ago.
So I praise God for His gifts
which He pours on us all
and drops after rain
whenever they fall.

Written on the same day as
"Leaves at Thanksgiving",
November 22, 2004.

## SHRINK NOT FROM THE HEIGHTS

The eagle shrinks not from the heights
nor do depths a fish dismay
and when obstacles arise for me
I will not turn away.
For as the eagle and the fish
suit well for sky and sea
so I find persistence
is a natural part of me.
For though sometimes defeated
I know not surrender
and so find victory ultimate
in its finest splendor.
And where I've fallen short
I cast a marker down –
Here I ventured unafraid
that I would crash or drown.
And from this place and time I see
that for my force of heart
where my mission ended
is, for someone else, a start
and a place to launch
a campaign of their own
for as a man does dare to dream
he does not dream alone.

# THE CONNECTION

There's a connection
between left brain and right
that opens a portal
in the dead of the night.
Logical thoughts
and imagination collide
touching each other
like the sand and the tide.
And raised from the deep
a mystery lies.
Walk on the beach
and open your eyes!
For what the tide carries
it carries away
and buries again
in the depths of the bay.
And only the pilgrim
who searches at dawn
will know of these things
before they are gone.
So attend to the stories
that the travelers tell
for their time and your time
are fleeting as well.

# VICTORY'S MOMENTS

Most often the reward
for a race well-run
is another stance
before a starting gun.
The competition's tougher
but I know that going in
and realize life gets harder
especially if I win.
For though a golden medal
around my neck be placed
it only takes one loss
for my fame to be erased.
But today I was the first
to cross the finish line
and no matter what else happens
that instant will be mine.
There's never rest for weary ones
and glory quickly fades
so treasure victory's moments
and not her accolades.
For it is in the striving
that victory is found
and in the pride that follows
she is so often bound.

# CHANGING TO JOY

When I offer to do
more than my part
in that very instant
there's a leap in my heart.
And suddenly I'm
a better man for
changing to joy
what once was a chore.
It's the one extra mile
when I'm dusty and tired
that transforms exhaustion
into a spirit inspired.
I'm a new person
for a deed kindly done
as with my commitment
I've already won.
Just a small burden
willingly lifted
and by the Spirit of God
I'm instantly gifted.
And I hope that it's this
that my fellow men see –
Jesus, my Savior,
working through me.

## IMAGINATION FINDS ME

I have followed this new path
for years and years it seems
and in so doing I have found
the source of all my dreams.
For I have had to trust
in a power more than man
one that when the best of us
says, "I can't!" it can.
I have had to leave to God
the ones who I love most
and so for my accomplishments
there is no call to boast.
There is a Spirit in the wind
and in my heart as well
that gives me words to say
and stories I must tell.
Imagination finds me
when I dare to pause
and from my busy day
the meaning of it draws.
And so I watch and wonder
as the ending nears
as from the haze that hides it
the light of truth appears.

# SPIDER IN THE WIND

I wonder at the spider
hanging in the wind.
On one remaining strand
does its presence here depend.
Buffeted by forces
that it cannot control
the spider clings with purpose
for rebuilding is its goal.
To start anew when all is lost,
the spider's set on spinning
as also is the watcher
who seeks a new beginning.
The spider and the dreamer
never count the cost.
As long as you believe
a dream is never lost.
The world will tear apart,
mock and taunt, destroy,
while the dreamer builds again
and fills his heart with joy.
For – lo! – the wind has died
and the spider spins anew
which I who watch and dream
will also surely do.

# THE BUTTERFLY BUILDER

Who would work so long a time
to build a butterfly
just to let it go
and watch it quickly die?
How could it be worth it
with such lowly compensation?
And what's the benefit
of human contemplation?
For as the flight of butterflies
is subject to the wind
so thoughts of individuals
come swiftly to an end.
Who will read and who will know
what I learned upon my way?
Yet on my walk I saw
a butterfly today.
Colors of the rainbow
sunlit through the wings!
I take joy in seeing
and writing of such things.
So I will build a butterfly
no matter what the cost
in hopes that its eternity
of beauty is not lost.

## MIRACLES AT NAIN

There was a miracle at Nain
the Bible tells about
and when Jesus raised the dead
there was a mighty shout!
"Here is God Almighty
standing next to me!"
Do I need a miracle
for I, the same, to see?
I do. And I have seen one.
Inside my heart, He reigns.
And every day's a miracle
that my Lord ordains.
For I was dead to sin
and now to life I'm raised.
And every day I'll lift my voice
in prayer that He be praised.
How many days are given
to walk upon the earth
and how few are those compared
to those with second birth?
Grieve not for the dead
who lay upon the bier.
A new child born of Jesus
in his place, stands here!

Luke 7:11-17

# TO RUN AND NOT BE WEARY

To run and not be weary,
to walk and not to faint,
these ideals are difficult
and that is my complaint.
I carry heavy loads
along the trail I tread
and I can't be bothered
with such thoughts up in my head.
Give me something practical
like a hammer or a nail.
It seems to me these things
weigh more on the scale.
I don't know how to use
the gifts that I receive
yet God will show me how
if I will just believe.
"A mustard seed of faith
is all it takes," said He,
amazing that the works of God
depend somehow on me.
A tiny step of faith
as I like Jesus act
and then the Holy Spirit
gives me what I lacked.
And now my breath is easy.
My feet are fast and light
as with the breath of God I run
with ne'er an end in sight.

# A SHIP AT SEA

I stand upon the deck
as though a ship at sea
for there are storms here on land
that toss and buffet me.
I set my feet apart
against the brimming tide
while my anger rises
from far down deep inside.
For I feel the current
and every wave and roll
and try to keep my feet
and mind in my control.
I cry out in the darkness,
"Lord, take me from this place!"
but He in greater wisdom
does fill me with His Grace.
And like the Sea of Galilee
where He did raise His hand
I find the storms that drive my life
react to His command.
For now the clouds have parted
and the sea is calm and still
as is my soul when it seeks
and acts within His will.

## TOUCHED BY THE EVENING BREEZE

I sit here in this same old place
I've sat time and time again
watching as the day does fade
and let the night sneak in.
I listen as the crickets chirp
and the birds sing evening song.
God's breath is in the breeze tonight
and here's where I belong.
Alone with Him just listening
to creation sing His praise
and I pray that He will grant me this
for all my earthly days:
A moment to reflect
and let my thoughts be calm
touched by evening breezes
resting safely in His palm.

Written July 16, 2004 in Forest Park.
I have had many more days to reflect.

# BENDING THE RAINBOW

Bright colors bending
so softly blending
in the rainbow that shines far above,
in silence I wonder
as I sit here far under
how this rainbow expresses God's love.
For I couldn't try
to reach colors so high
as beautiful as they all might be,
but bending down like the rain
God makes it plain
that He's the One reaching to me.
The meaning I catch
is if I'd only stretch
my finger that He'd do the rest,
but He's already done it
through Jesus His Son. It
is just as the Gospels attest.
What did I learn?
It's a love I can't earn!
But I can gather it as it descends.
So I'll catch each and all
of the colors that fall
and thank God for the rainbow He bends.

## FOR GRANTED

Do I take for granted
the gift You've given me
though it cost You everything
since it was mine for free?
Do I forget the sacrifice
that You so bravely made
when You Your life of righteousness
for mine of sin did trade?
How can I so glibly
of salvation speak
when I know the evil things
that my heart does seek?
Do You want that I
should suffer just as You?
I simply am not able
to drink the cup You drew.
Oh, how full You know me
in my weakness and my sin!
Yet every time I fall
You lift me up again
not expecting strength
of body but of love
that flows in endless portion
when I lift my eyes above.
"Take my gift with joy!
Be thankful and be brave
and pass the word to others
whom I have yet to save.
A gift is not a gift
if it comes with guilt
for it is on joy and freedom
My Holy Kingdom's built.
I have made you worthy
as children of the King!

It is your love He treasures
so that offering to Him bring
not with thoughts of sorrow
but with bright and happy song
for love so freely given
thrives forever long."

I have been writing poems
and publishing books since 2002.

## MORE THAN WIND OR WINGS

I remember that first morning
when I wobbled to the edge.
If my parents hadn't nudged me
I'd still be on that ledge!
I wonder how they knew
these wings of mine would hold.
Without their love to nurture me
I'd have never been so bold.
And others gave me counsel
and help upon my way.
Their many acts of friendship
helped get me here today.
And here I am at last
with wings upon the wind
certain in the knowledge
on these I can depend:
Loyalty and kindness,
the wonder of God's grace,
vision, opportunity,
and courage to give chase.
The love of all my family
and good wishes from my friends,
a nation built on freedom:
These are lifting winds.
And my wings no longer tremble.
They are filled with Godly might!
This more than the wind or wings
gives me eagle's flight.

## REFLECTIONS OF WINGS

Reflections of wings
on a clear mountain pond
remind me of times
when I reached beyond
the bonds and the limits
the world placed on me
and how great and how glorious
it feels to be free.
It's easy for an eagle
to soar and to fly
over the mountaintops!
And in my heart so can I!
For there is no obstacle
known to man or to beast
that Spirit can't conquer
and the least
I can do
in this earthly disguise
is ask God for direction
then lift up my eyes,
not to the mountaintops
or the stars or the sun,
but straight to His glory
and the battle is won!
Reflections of wings
on this tiny lake
are both sign and symbol
of the journey I take
and from those reflections
at the edge of this pond
the day of my spirit
has suddenly dawned.

## PURPLE AT DAWN

Orange at sunset,
purple at dawn,
with the brightest of colors
our lives are drawn.
Green leaves in springtime,
yellow in fall,
God gives them life
and colors them all.
Stars in the heavens
reflect in the sea,
God in His glory
yet reaching for me.
Why am I burdened
with doubts and with fear
when God makes it apparent
that He's always near?
A rainbow, a sunbeam,
a bird on the wing –
love unsurpassed
from Jesus the King –
and like the sun rising
or falling away
these I will use
to color my day.

# THE LAST BASTION

Little things distract me
from the big ones occurring
but changes are coming
that will be enduring.
Democracy is
under attack
as into the darkness
the world's being drawn back.
Try to protect it
with barriers and walls
as each who does not
one by one falls.
Yet the storm that approaches
is so powerfully vast
that even the bastion
will crack from the blast.
The only One stronger
then the storm is the King
the God of the Cosmos
Who made everything.
He is the refuge
for both body and soul
so into His shelter
as the warning bells toll.
For though death is certain
in all people's fates
the kingdom of heaven
for His children awaits.

## JUSTICE, PEACE AND MERCY

It is right to demand
justice for the dead
and yet the price is not less peace
but more of it instead.
For there can be no justice
in a fracas or a fight
as decisions won by battle
depend alone on might.
Peace is thus prerequisite
for justice to prevail
and if there is no mercy
even peace will fail.
But how can one be merciful
when no one can agree
on what is just and what is not?
There is no guarantee.
The only thing that's sure
is that every generation
will find itself engaged
in some conflagration.
The only route to justice
depends on finding peace
which relies itself on mercy
so it's love that must increase.
The powers of this world
would drive us all apart
and with hatred's hammer strike
the love from every heart.
We are Adam's seed
each and every one
trying to claim God's power
with each rising sun.
But God is God and man is man
who challenges God's will

trying to decide for Him
who He'll let live or kill.
It's mercy, peace and love
that justice is defending
for without these there is none
in a cycle never-ending.
"No peace. No justice."
Write the signs that way
and offer love and mercy
when you go out today.

Sometimes a poem can help to create understanding
where there was none.  And in that spirit this poem
was written on July 9, 2016.

## AN INNOCENT MAN

I am a criminal
according to them
the same ones who struck
and crucified Him.
What kind of justice
accepts such a wrong?
I am convicted
for I'm weak and they're strong.
And were I the master
and they were the slave
I'd see that they'd suffer
the same as they gave.
For I am no better
and I am no worse
than those who afflict me.
That's man's constant curse.
There's no way around it
as with hatred I'm filled
for the way of the world
is kill or be killed.
Yet there is a man
who hangs beside me
who from this cruel cycle
is apparently free.
I hear Him speaking
to God as His Son
and it's clear He is here
for the things that I've done.
He could come down
but for Mercy He stays
and for me and our killers
in Kindness He prays.
I'm overcome
with tears not of pain
for a Spirit now fills me
that I cannot explain.
In agony's midst
I feel Comfort and Peace

sure of Salvation
when my struggles here cease.
For I offered my heart
here in the end
and Jesus declared me
both Brother and Friend.
And as brother and friend
to you now I speak.
Here is the change
in the world that you seek.
For I no longer follow
the kill or killed law.
From His infinite Love
I now constantly draw.
An innocent man
on this cross here hung high
for the blood of my Savior
before God am I.

# PERHAPS IT WAS

Sometimes it is useful
to take some time to pause
before one spends one's money
or time upon a cause.
I spent all my life
working and believing
while others did much better
lying and deceiving.
I sought the best in man
who so often disappointed
and hated me for seeming
to think I was anointed.
And if it seemed that way
perhaps 'twas because 'twas true
for God gave me a calling
and a mission I must do.
And to be successful
I must seek Him every day
knowing He will guide me
safely on my way.

Written on September 7, 2016.
May God guide and protect you on your way as well

# THE PREY OF TIME

The day of expectations
has quickly come and gone.
Sunrise leads to sunset
which yields again to dawn –
Glorious days of youth
and dreams to fill the skies,
a young man who now wears
an older one's disguise.
The promise of my dreams,
how can I fulfill?
I still don't have the answer
and suppose I never will.
I'm such a little man
in such a giant place,
a prey to time except
for God's Almighty Grace.
It fills me up and makes me
powerful yet mild,
the present of a Father
surrendered to His child.
It pours out of me
as enduring rhyme
and thus I am the master
and not the prey of time.

## STILL IT SURPRISES

It rustles the leaves
as it quickly arises.
I hear its advance
yet still it surprises.
Cool and relaxing
with its sweet caress
it carries the scent
of the roses to bless.
Invisible yet
I can't live without air.
Through what it provides
I know it is there.
More than life by itself
in the sweet summer breeze,
joy, awe and wonder –
yes, it brings me these.
And just how much greater
is the God Who I serve
to bless me much more
than I'd ever deserve?
So I sit and I listen
to the life-giving wind
and to the Spirit of God
on Whom I depend.

# INTERVENE

Lord I pray
Intervene.
Take me from
This sordid scene.
Raise and lift
Me above
Surrounded by
Your mighty love.
Body, spirit,
Mind of mine,
Change to holy
And divine.
What I ask,
All I need,
Let me be
A thriving seed,
One from which
Fruit doth grow
So others, too,
May come to know
You as Savior,
Lord and King
Which is really
Everything.

## Alphabetical List of Poems

$9.95
ISBN 978-0-9910804-2-7
5 0 9 9 5 >

9 780991 080427